Hello,
You're Fabulous!

SANDY SLOVACK, M.A.

BALBOA.
PRESS
A DIVISION OF HAY HOUSE

Balboa Press books may be ordered through booksellers or by contacting:

Balboa Press
A Division of Hay House
1663 Liberty Drive
Bloomington, IN 47403
www.balboapress.com
1 (877) 407-4847

Because of the dynamic nature of the Internet, any web addresses or links contained in this book may have changed since publication and may no longer be valid. The views expressed in this work are solely those of the author and do not necessarily reflect the views of the publisher, and the publisher hereby disclaims any responsibility for them.

The author of this book does not dispense medical advice or prescribe the use of any technique as a form of treatment for physical, emotional, or medical problems without the advice of a physician, either directly or indirectly. The intent of the author is only to offer information of a general nature to help you in your quest for emotional and spiritual well-being. In the event you use any of the information in this book for yourself, which is your constitutional right, the author and the publisher assume no responsibility for your actions.

Print information available on the last page.

ISBN: 978-1-5043-3457-0 (sc)
ISBN: 978-1-5043-3459-4 (hc)
ISBN: 978-1-5043-3458-7 (e)

Library of Congress Control Number: 2015909865

Balboa Press rev. date: 07/30/2015

CONTENTS

There is no better day than today to feel great about you! Remove any hint of poor self-esteem and rewrite the stories that have been holding you back from the success, joy and abundance that you so deserve. At last, a book that'll show you how!

Through the processes in this book, you will:

- Identify the beliefs you have about yourself that hold you back and learn how to change them.
- Experience life with a new sense of excitement and passion.
- Count on yourself more and call yourself 'friend.'
- Improve your relationships.
- Have more energy, enthusiasm, and zest for life.
- Notice others treat you better & treat yourself better.
- Find life easier, sleep better, and have more fun.
- Manage stress more effectively.
- Have a profoundly positive impact on the world around you.
- Feel deserving of love, joy and laughter and experience more of these each day.

ABOUT THE AUTHOR

I wrote this book originally in 2008 and was in the process of publishing it when I had a brain tumour suddenly diagnosed and removed a year in October of 2013. One of my favorite quotes is "Live as though you'll die tomorrow and learn as if you'll live forever." The more I understand about me and this magnificent universe I live in, the juicier life gets! Since my surgery, this has become especially true!

I have worked as a Clinical Counsellor since I earned my Masters degree in 1995 and I have been working in the helping profession for more than 35 years. My area of expertise has been working with people dealing with the effects of trauma. During the last many years, I had worked in the Mental Health and Addictions field with both adults and youth. I love seeing people get past their 'stuff' and find joy and well being in their lives!

There is something magical about witnessing people remembering and 'soaking in' their own value. It is incredible to then watch, as people get excited about, and then teach others, to do the same. I have built a great reputation as a trainer and speaker because my work has been such a joy!

With my experience, in combination with my tremendous energy and passion for helping you to re-discover your authentic worth, I promise that you will see great results! On the journey we will laugh a lot and have a blast. I am interested in possibility, inspiration and in witnessing you create amazing success according to how YOU define that.

I have my 'story' to tell, as we all do. When it comes to understanding how to build self-esteem, I've not only helped hundreds of others, but I've learned how to do this for myself from the rock bottom up to the sky. If I can do it, anybody can; and I will show you how!

I have written articles, workbooks, and I offer keynotes, coaching sessions, webinars/tele-seminars and live workshops. I'm thrilled that you have found this book, congratulations for investing in you! We're going to have a blast!

Here's to your magnificence!

FOREWORD

Sometimes there are moments in our lives when we meet someone and our intuition about them and what they are capable of creating screams at us like a siren in the night.

That's what happened when I first met Sandy.

To be honest, I don't even remember what Passion Test Certification Program she was attending, or the first conversation we had, but I definitely remember the feeling I had when I met her.

It was one big KABOOM!

Sandy's presence was so powerful that I had to step back and take a deep breath. A chuckle, immediately following my inhale, ran completely through me. "Oh my God"…I thought…exhaling… Sandy is a "unique to serve." Yeah!

A "unique to serve" is someone that I have coined who is on this planet to teach all of us, just by their mere presence, what the words "mission and purpose" look like in action.

From the moment we met, I could sense that Sandy would not only do whatever she was here to do with 'style and panache,' but that she would also do it with excellence!!

Oh how I love being right!

In Sandy's new book, '**Hello, You're Fabulous!**' she has done what many authors attempt to do, but don't. In her breezy, easy, down to earth, say it like it is style, Sandy has created an incredibly simple yet profound book that not only takes the reader on a magical journey of their own inner self discovery, but she also gives them a profound, yet practical road map filled with deep insights, wisdom and the prescriptions they need to raise what she cleverly calls their "Vibration Meter."

As I was reading all about her "Vibration Meter," I automatically started thinking, "Hmmm, what am I currently vibrating at?!"

Bingo…She had me!

Seriously…Since everyone and everything are affected in our lives by where we're at, wouldn't you agree that it's really important to be conscious about where you're vibrating on your Vibration Meter and to keep raising your vibration level?

As Sandy says, and I quote: "If my Vibration Meter is currently at low, I will be attracting things, situations, and people that are a vibrational match to that."

Vibration Meter

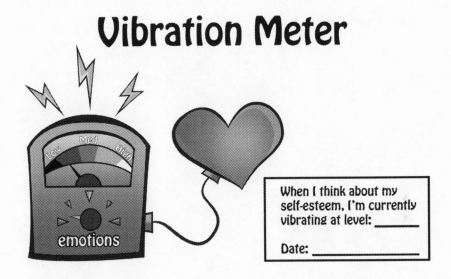

When I think about my self-esteem, I'm currently vibrating at level: _____

Date: _____

I kept reading on and on and with each chapter I was more and more excited. The clarity with which Sandy unveils the different pitfalls and challenges that can lead to one's lack of self esteem, and then with the same crystal clear clarity how she illustrates and gives do-able and easy to follow prescriptions that each of us can easily incorporate into our lives, was brilliant!

Congratulations for finding your way into Sandy's world and welcome to a journey of self-discovery that will bring you more good than you could ever imagine!!

Janet Bray Attwood is the New York Times Bestselling Co-author, "The Passion Test – the Effortless Path to Discovering Your Life Purpose"

Section 1

Section

If you've ever felt low or down on yourself (and who hasn't), you may not think it's very easy to simply change your belief system to thinking and *believing*, "I'm a worthwhile and lovable person." That's what self-esteem is, it's about how I feel about me; it's my belief in my own value. Thinking about self-esteem in the context of the Law of Attraction may help that shift to seem easier.

I have spent many years in the vicious cycle of thinking poorly of myself and creating more negativity because of where I was focused. The big question, then, is "How do I break the cycle?" I was in a pretty big pit that I had created and the prospect of getting out of it felt quite hopeless and overwhelming.

Learning about the Law of Attraction is what made the difference in my life and how I experience the world. The most straightforward definition of the Law of Attraction that I have come across is by the author, Michael Losier:

> *I attract to my life whatever I give my energy, focus and attention to, whether wanted or unwanted.*

The Law of Attraction is far more to me than 'positive thinking,' which is what I hear some people reduce it to. It's trickier than that… I actually have to *believe* my positive thoughts and be in the good energy of those thoughts to manifest positive results.

If I have low self-esteem and suddenly I want to believe I'm great, my odds are not great at buying in. Use the exercises in this book to start small and build your way up. Find evidence that there are things about you that you do believe in. My guess is that things get missed or taken for granted.

Given that the Law of Attraction is about what I am focused on, this is not about 'suddenly being great' at all. It's about rediscovering what is already great about me, focusing on that (instead of what I don't like about me) and believing that having more self-worth is possible. Believing, trusting, imagining and holding that vision is the essence of self-confidence.

To have self-confidence is to know that I have something to offer the world and others; it's an assurance that I'm not only OK, but I have value to contribute. To have confidence is a belief or a trust in who I am.

What exactly is a belief anyway? Well, a belief is simply a thought that I keep on thinking; it's a pattern in my brain that I believe to be true. There is no 'truth' for everyone, truth is an opinion or a pattern which I continue to find affirming evidence of because I am expecting a certain result. Something is 'true' because I am looking for it to be so; I continue to find the same results repeatedly to create a belief.

We are thus the creators of our own experience or perspective of the world. Once I am aware of this I am in a far better position to be creating my 'truth' or experience in the world the way I'd like to be. In order to become more aware, I'd like to invite you to spend some time getting conscious of some of the 'truths' that you currently hold and likely have had since childhood.

Like most people, I learned to think from a negative perspective before I had language for it - as a very small child. I figured out there was a correlation between my behaviour and other people's reactions to me. If I spilled milk and got yelled at, it makes sense that my conclusion at the time would have been that I was 'bad' or, at the very least, at some sort of 'fault'. I made up in my mind that how others reacted to me was about what I did and, even further, it was about me and who I am at my core.

The truth at the time was that I was a small child learning about my environment and about motor skills. I was learning and discovering my world as perfectly as any child does. In fact, that was my job as a young child, to be an impressionable sponge and learn to make connections.

What was actually out of place was being yelled at due to an adult's impatience, which is really all about them. I would guess that I must have felt confused at the time and, like any child might do, I made it about me.

It was about me because at that stage of development, everything IS about me. We are just learning how to interact and know about 'others'. I came into this world, as we all did, with an open and trusting spirit. As a sponge, I absorbed every message that I was given. Many of those messages were not so blatant but subtle and tough to even identify.

Developmental psychology explains that most of what I know about the world was cemented in me before I was about eight years old. How I feel about me, relationships, money, trust, communication, adults, sharing… all of it was unconsciously operating in me by that very young age. I took cues by watching my parents, other adults, other kids, TV, and anywhere that there was messaging about how the world worked.

I accepted what I heard and saw as the 'truth' about how human beings worked. Each of us learn very different messages in these years and each of us has our own version of the 'truth' that is unique to us. I have been proving to myself that I've been right about my 'truth' for years. The evidence that I've been expecting to find is what I have been open to finding and, therefore, exactly what I find. In my case, I continued to find evidence that I was not a worthy person. There seemed to be no shortage of that evidence either.

How many of you have ever been in a store and heard a small child say "I want that" to a parent to then hear the parent say "You don't deserve that" or "You're too fat" or even "Don't be stupid"? Listening to messaging like this as a child teaches a child about his or her value; it creates poor self-esteem.

Not all of the messaging is so blatantly obvious though. Some of the messaging is very well intended toward keeping a child safe, for example. I hear parents saying "Stay away from the edge of the pool Stevie, it's very dangerous" and then they wonder why Stevie is deathly afraid of the water and feels less than capable later on in swim class.

Swimming, by the way, happens to be one of the abilities that human beings have naturally at birth. We can swim instinctively, just like dolphins, by lying on our backs and breathing. It is as instinctual as suckling for milk. How many people do you know who have learned to believe that they can't swim or who are afraid of the water?

On the following pages, give thoughtful responses in completing the exercise on Beliefs & Truths. The first thought that enters your mind is usually accurate. The beliefs that we have are so ingrained that we don't even realize they may be different from what others believe. Write down whatever comes to you about the given topic.

For example, regarding money, I may believe that "I have to work hard to get money". For others, "Money comes easily to me and it is simply a tool that is used toward creating more flow of it". There are no right or wrong answers here.

Beliefs & 'Truths' about how the world worked:

By watching your parents or care providers, other adults, other kids, TV, teachers, coaches, reading magazines, etc. Think about and write down the beliefs do you currently have about each of the following topics:

Relationships

_____

_____

_____

_____

_____

_____

_____

Communication

_____

_____

_____

_____

_____

_____

Showing Your Feelings

_____

_____

_____

_____

_____

_____

Showing Affection

_____

_____

_____

_____

_____

_____

Problem solving

_____
_____
_____
_____
_____
_____
_____

Money

_____
_____
_____
_____
_____
_____

Work

_____
_____
_____
_____
_____
_____

Time

_____
_____
_____
_____
_____
_____
_____

Family

_____
_____
_____
_____
_____
_____
_____

Commitment

_____
_____
_____
_____
_____
_____
_____

Men

_____

_____

_____

_____

_____

_____

_____

Women

_____

_____

_____

_____

_____

_____

Religion/Spirituality

_____

_____

_____

_____

_____

_____

My Own Value

_____

_____

_____

_____

_____

_____

_____

Being 'In the Vibe'

Given that we are all forms of energy, we all have an energetic 'vibration'. That is to say, every one of our thoughts and feelings offer a vibrational frequency out into the universe.

As stated before, our 'truths' or our pattern of beliefs are created by what we draw our attention to and, therefore, find evidence of. What we attract is at the same vibrational frequency to where we are; we attract people, places and events that are a vibrational match to us.

We have made something 'true' because we have offered a vibration on that frequency. Since we are doing this, whether we realize it or not (consciously or subconsciously), let's do this on purpose and create a 'reality' that we actually want.

So, how do I do that? Well, human beings were designed with a built in 'Vibration Meter' and, if you're anything like me, you just didn't know that for a long time. They are called *feelings (or emotions)*. I've always known that I could feel lousy or great, but it was never clear that my feelings were my clue as to what direction to take.

When my life was not working the way I wanted it to, I was feeling bad and that is a 'vibrational match'. When I feel great about me and my life, I raise my vibrational frequency and become a match to the great life that I then attract. Sounds simple, right? Well, let's break it down even more...

You can tell what level you are vibrating at in each life category by how you feel when you think about it. Imagine that you have a meter that is plugged in to your feelings about your own value. If you feel down, you are on the low end of the 'Vibration Meter'. If you feel hopeful, that's a big improvement in energy over feeling down. It still may not be totally comfortable or where you want to be, and it is higher on the meter toward joy.

As you think about your self-esteem, give yourself a current rating of your level of vibration.

Vibration Meter

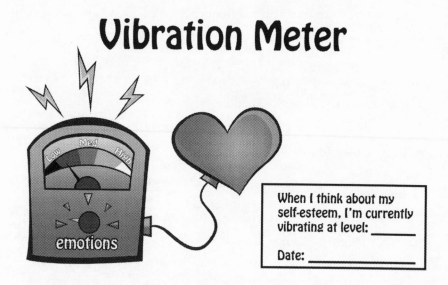

When I think about my self-esteem, I'm currently vibrating at level: _____

Date: _____

Another way to know what level of vibration you are at is to look at how your life is working out for you. If my 'Vibration Meter' is currently at low, I will be attracting things, situations, and people that are a vibrational match to that.

It is impossible to create great results when you feel lousy; there is no vibrational match or 'alignment' with how I feel. All we need to know about how to improve our lives is how to be in alignment with a higher level of vibration. The rest of this book will walk you through how to do that.

Alignment with My Magnificence

Ultimately, my goal is to be in alignment with who I really am. If you are discovering that you are rating lower than you'd like to be on the meter, it isn't because you deserve to feel bad. Quite the contrary, it is only because you are out of alignment with who you really are.

When we begin our journey into this world, as early as when in the womb, we are in perfect alignment with a perfect or high vibration. How we are meant to feel and who we are at our fundamental core is magnificent!

Paying attention to our emotions is how we can measure our alignment with our fundamental self-worth. When I feel great, my meter is reading high and this means that I am in vibrational alignment to my true self-worth. The second I feel sadness or any negative emotion, it means that I am out of alignment with who I'm meant to be.

The Main Premise

What I am inviting you to consider is the idea that you are, at your core, a whole, healthy, brilliant bundle of magnificent and radiant brilliance. Through the process of this book, you will be able to remember that and feel that.

Inherent to this idea is the knowledge that you manifest your experience of life. This is great information to have because, what that means, is that you have the power and ability to manifest magnificence!

What About Being a Realist?

'Reality' is simply that which we hold to be true about what 'real' is. There was a long time in my life when I would have laughed if you told me I was magnificent. I believed it could be true for others… but certainly not for me. I was very much out of alignment with my true self and that is the reality that I had created for myself at the time.

These ideas of being magnificent may sound great if you are willing to entertain the possibility that it's possible that this is so. I remember having a really tough time with this because I didn't like to be wrong in my life. It is possible that you just don't buy this 'magnificent' premise because it's too far-fetched too.

If you are in that position (like I was) I'd like you to consider the list of beliefs that you wrote out earlier. Ask yourself how the beliefs that you currently have are working out for you so far. Chances are, you could do with raising your vibration level up a notch at the very least (feel better), so hang in there with me.

I'm not asking you to take on this main premise as a belief or as your 'truth' right now. I'm asking you to try this on for a while and suspend what disbelief may be lingering for a time. Practice these concepts a bit and remain open to the possibility that you could feel better about yourself and your world.

If you are ever tempted to say, "Oh, forget it" through this process, it only means you are about to step into some unfamiliar ground or into some resistance. We will work with that; it's a valuable part of the process.

I want you to feel fabulous about you, just like you deserve to. I am so thankful that I learned to create the 'reality' that I live in now. There were times when I felt so bad about me that I didn't believe I deserved to live! Is it time for you to choose to create a new reality?

All that I have loved deeply becomes a part of me; it is still in me to access, even if I don't remember it at this moment. All that I have enjoyed, valued and loved is forever mine to keep!

Pay Attention to How You *Feel*

The first step toward realigning with my magnificence, or vibrating at a higher frequency, is to practice paying attention to how I feel. In the teachings of Abraham, they might say something like "Reach for a better feeling thought". Well, "That's easy to say," is what I remember thinking when I first heard that sort of statement. Before I could start feeling better, I realized that I needed to learn to become aware of what I was feeling to begin with.

What I noticed was that, as I had conversations during my day, I would continue to repeat stories that reinforced 'being right' about how lousy I felt. I was actually shocked at how any times I got others to listen to me complain about my situation, about my job, the government, money, other people, etc. I started to notice the feeling that I had in my body during the course of my days. The overwhelming majority of the time, I spent my energy in negative emotion; cut off from my magnificence. I hadn't even realized this!

As humans, we like to be right and there was a lot of juice in this pattern of thought and negative emotion for me. I was right, but I sure wasn't happy. So, rather than making myself 'wrong' (because there really is no wrong way to do life), I decided what I'd rather be right about. That gave me different topics to focus on in my day.

Section 1 Assignment

1. As you notice yourself in conversation over the next week, notice what your predominant feeling is. Notice the topics you choose to engage in.
    - Are you complaining?
    - Are your reiterating the reasons and excuses about why you don't have what you want?
    - Are you being 'right' about beliefs that no longer serve you?
    - Do you spend time defending your 'reality' or wondering how to be creating a new one?

    Choose topics that feel better. Catch yourself when you are complaining and stop. Then think about something you appreciate about the same situation.

    For example, if you are complaining about the weather, think of something that you appreciate about the current conditions.

    This exercise is simply intended to increase your level of awareness about how you are feeling as you go through the day.

2. Begin creating an 'Appreciation List'. On the following page, begin listing things that you appreciate in your life. It's impossible to feel bad when I am in a state of appreciation. Add more things daily and spend time every morning reviewing it to start your day. There's no better way to begin the day's vibration than from a place of appreciation!

3. On the following pages, begin to create new beliefs that work for you. Review the list of beliefs that you have had up until now, in the earlier exercise, and rewrite beliefs that you would rather have.

It's OK if your new beliefs don't feel true right now. That comes with repetition, practice and finding evidence. This is about bringing to your awareness things that you **DO** want; beliefs that will feel good to you (when you do really believe them).

My Appreciation List

Cuddling my cat
The smell of rain
Hugging my

My *NEW* Beliefs & 'Truths' about how the world works:

What would you ***rather*** think about each of these topics? Think about what you deserve in your core, when you are connected to your magnificence.

Relationships

_____

_____

_____

_____

_____

_____

Communication

_____

_____

_____

_____

_____

_____

Showing Feelings

_____

_____

_____

_____

_____

_____

_____

Showing Affection

_____

_____

_____

_____

_____

_____

Problem solving

_____

_____

_____

_____

_____

_____

Money

_____

_____

_____

_____

_____

_____

_____

Work

_____

_____

_____

_____

_____

_____

Time

_____

_____

_____

_____

_____

_____

Family

_____

_____

_____

_____

_____

_____

_____

Commitment

_____

_____

_____

_____

_____

_____

_____

Men

_____

_____

_____

_____

_____

_____

_____

Women

_____
_____
_____
_____
_____
_____
_____

Religion/Spirituality

_____
_____
_____
_____
_____
_____
_____

My Own Value

_____
_____
_____
_____
_____
_____
_____

Section 2

Section 2

Facing 'Reality'

The last section talked a little bit about reality; looking at your current beliefs and beginning to think about what you may rather believe. This section is about putting an end to 'facing reality' toward creating it.

By now you are far more aware of the thoughts and feelings that create your dominant vibration out there. If you're anything like me, you might be saying, "I get it but I don't know how to change it." This is perfectly OK. In fact, getting clear about what you don't want is a very helpful thing toward getting clear about what you *do* want.

Your Wish is Law of Attraction's Command

Every time we are in a situation that we don't like, we naturally develop a desire for what we do want. We are in a universe that grows and expands. Whatever we focus on grows and whatever we can imagine is possible.

So, if I don't feel worthy, I want to feel worthy. The universal Law of Attraction energy hears my request to feel more worthy and automatically responds with a "yes". It then manifests the ways and means for me to collect what I desire - to feel worthy.

Just like that, **POOF!** , done. No exceptions.

Whatever I can imagine or wish or desire I can create and turn into a reality. Rather than being frustrated about things not working out for me now, I think about what I want and look forward to it happening.

The part where most people get stuck (and boy, did I get stuck!) is in *believing* that whatever I want is right there for the receiving. I didn't know how to let it in. I really wanted to believe that it was all there for me, but it would have meant giving up literally years of what I had known to be true about me… that I didn't matter; that I wasn't worthy of having it. My beliefs were pretty ingrained.

Think back over the past week. Think about the negative beliefs you have that you really wanted to dig your heels in about. What is it that keeps us wanting to be so right about stuff that feels so bad? What is it with that?

"Start the Car!"

Imagine that moment when you get an unexpected surprise or gift as simple as a compliment. What do you do with it in your heart and in your mind? This is an opportunity to stare boldly into the belief you have about your value, and receive what you are actually worthy of. To have a solid sense of self worth is to say "Thank you." How many of us really allow that to happen; to really be open to feeling acknowledged for who we are? Let's face it… it's a process.

First you may go into shock and disbelief, like the woman in the Ikea commercial who looks at her receipt and can't believe the amazing bargain she's getting. She figures it must be a mistake and that she had better get out of there before they discover their error.

Running out of the store like a panicked fugitive attempting to stay calm, she yells to her awaiting accomplice (I'm guessing her husband)

"Start the car!" She doesn't actually believe it's real; she thinks she's cheating some system to get a good deal.

It is with this same sense of disbelief that I have often walked through the world. I haven't always expected to be treated kindly and when I am, it can be difficult to believe, acknowledge or accept, let alone allow it to be about what I deserve in the world.

Sometimes I think that I've somehow fooled the system, as in the Ikea commercial, and I really don't allow myself to receive any acknowledgement that is positive because I have not bought into the idea that I truly have value. I deflect recognition and compliments rather than allow them to validate what is really true about me (and of all of us) - that I have tremendous value.

Changing My Mind

It's not anyone's 'fault' that I have poor self-esteem. Even if I can see where my messaging came from, it is ultimately me who bought in to the notion that I was not valuable or lovable somehow. This isn't about parents being 'bad' or 'wrong' and it is also not about me being 'bad' or 'wrong' either. I can say, "Wow, I bought into that," simply for what it was - a story about me that was made up.

Whether it was made up in my head or whether someone else gave me the idea that I was not worthy, it is still simply a story; a belief; an idea or an opinion. In recognizing that, I have an opportunity to choose to tell myself a different story and actually start thinking something else.

My 'truth' today that, I have tremendous value; that I believe in my 'main premise' and in my magnificence, is simply that... a story. But, this story serves me, and those around me, better. It's a story I'd rather believe.

To change my mind is a game of consciousness. I had never thought that all my beliefs were 'stories' until it was brought to my attention. The more aware I became of the stories that I carried around in my head, the easier it was to catch myself playing the 'old tapes' running in my head and, thus, being in a position to create new tapes today.

It is important then to be aware of what my stories are about my self-worth. Do I believe I'm a worthy, lovable person? The fact is that I could find lots of 'evidence' to support both how worthy or how rotten I was. It depended entirely on what information I was choosing to focus on, and it was typically the negative stuff.

Finding the Evidence

We can actually redesign beliefs when we can identify what they are. When you can see the evidence that you can change a belief, you will find it easier to change many more toward having the rich and full life that you deserve.

Also, when I change one belief in one area, this will have an impact on other areas. For example, if I change a belief about money, this may have an impact on a belief I have about work.

Think over the past week now and look for things that you noticed as exceptions in your old thinking patterns and beliefs.

In each category that you wrote new beliefs for, can you find a few pieces of evidence that support your new belief? Review your 'NEW Beliefs' notes from the last section and document evidence that your new beliefs are 'True'. Write down times that you remember feeling prosperous, positive about relationships, having moments when things went smoothly, you were communicating well with people, etc. If you don't find evidence, write about evidence you **will** find in the coming week.

Evidence of My New Beliefs & 'Truths':

Relationships

_____

_____

_____

_____

_____

_____

Communication

_____

_____

_____

_____

_____

_____

Showing Feelings

_____

_____

_____

_____

_____

_____

Showing Affection

_____

_____

_____

_____

_____

_____

_____

Problem solving

_____

_____

_____

_____

_____

_____

Money

_____

_____

_____

_____

_____

Work

_____
_____
_____
_____
_____
_____
_____

Time

_____
_____
_____
_____
_____
_____
_____

Family

_____
_____
_____
_____
_____
_____
_____

Commitment

_____

_____

_____

_____

_____

_____

_____

Men

_____

_____

_____

_____

_____

_____

Women

_____

_____

_____

_____

_____

_____

_____

Religion/Spirituality

_____

_____

_____

_____

_____

_____

My Own Value

_____

_____

_____

_____

_____

_____

Take a moment to focus on the evidence that things are working well and that you are 'right' about beliefs that are positive and affirming. Notice that it feels good.

The secret that I've discovered for myself is… there's actually nothing easier than feeling good. Even if it sounds scary or hard, once I decided to allow myself a different opinion, life felt much, much easier… because it is. Feeling lousy is energy draining and all consuming, isn't it? Having my old beliefs was a hard road.

I had grown accustomed to thinking about my 'tragic' past and I was focused on how rotten some of my experiences were. In many ways, how lousy I felt about me became a large part of my identity, meaning, I hung around others who felt the same way. This reinforced my low self-esteem in a big way.

One of the old beliefs that I discovered I had was that self-confidence was the same as arrogance. This one was sneaky and I really wasn't aware that I had it until I dug a little deeper. I asked myself what was going on that I was stuck in the belief that I wasn't OK. That's when I discovered the fear that I would be seen as arrogant if I felt good.

I didn't want to be arrogant. I gave that energy and, low and behold, I was arrogant for a very long time. My arrogance was my insecurity pretending to be secure. My false image is what perpetuated my low self-esteem.

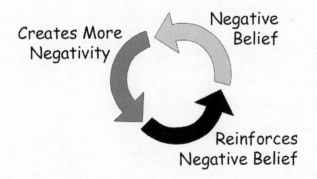

Clearly, there were prices that I was paying (big time) for being right about being worthless. What I started to think about though was what I had invested in it. What was I getting out of holding on to this belief that wasn't serving me? Well, it was easier than changing, for one. I got attention (even if it was negative). I didn't have to accomplish much because I didn't expect it of myself. I could go on and on.

Some examples of your costs or the prices that you might be paying for being right about having low self-value are:

⇒ *I feel stuck*
⇒ *I'm surrounded with others who are low energy*
⇒ *Relationships with my family have suffered*
⇒ *I'm in a job I hate*
⇒ *I have no money*
⇒ *I put up with poor treatment from others*

Write your list of prices or costs that you are paying for being right about having low self-value:

⇒ _____
⇒ _____
⇒ _____
⇒ _____
⇒ _____
⇒ _____
⇒ _____
⇒ _____
⇒ _____
⇒ _____
⇒ _____
⇒ _____

Feeling Better is the Key to Feeling Great!

If what I focus on grows, then I want to focus on feeling better than how I feel now. You may have built a lifetime of evidence to prove to yourself that you don't have value. It may take some time (or not, you get to pick) but you can find all the evidence you need to prove yourself right about being an amazing, wonderful, valuable, magnificent and lovable human being too.

Take a moment to think about how it might feel to like yourself. This may be a stretch for some of you and easy for others. Imagine what would be different if you really felt great about who you are: confident, strong and vibrant.

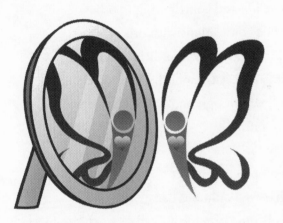

Rather than focusing on what you *don't* have or the prices you've paid, let's focus on what you *want,* and expect that it will occur. Look at the list below. Even if some of these seem out of reach in the moment, check the signs of great self-esteem that are currently true for you.

Notice what it feels like to check the ones you already have, and imagine what it will feel like when you have them all.

Checklist for Signs of Great Self-Esteem:

- I take time for self care ('me-time' activities)
- I am gentle and appreciate my environment
- I am self nurturing
- I give care and attention to my appearance
- I feel healthy, eat well and remain active
- I enjoying friends & social activities
- I enjoy and accept compliments openly
- I experience joy regularly
- I spend time being in appreciation
- I feel abundant
- I love life and contributing to others
- I value connections with others
- I find it easy to ask for help or support
- I am appreciative of others' perspective
- I follow through on my commitments
- I am on time
- I have lots of energy
- I am open and present
- I share my opinions constructively
- I feel empowered from a place of choice in my life
- I am in relationships with healthy people
- I appreciate and honour my accomplishments and strengths
- I share the 'good news' with others
- I love myself

Take a moment to look again at this Checklist. Notice how it feels to have checked signs that are currently true for you and imagine what it will feel like when you have them all. Then, answer the following questions as specifically as you can...

When you imagine being completely aligned with your magnificence and you are feeling fabulous about you...

(Spend some time with this!)
What would your friends and family notice about you?

_____

_____

_____

_____

_____

_____

_____

What would others see when watching you walking down the street?

_____

_____

_____

_____

_____

_____

_____

What would you be doing?

_____

_____

_____

_____

_____

_____

_____

How would you feel about your relationships?

_____

_____

_____

_____

_____

_____

What would you be talking about?

_____

_____

_____

_____

_____

_____

What kinds of events would you be planning or looking forward to?

_____

_____

_____

_____

_____

_____

_____

Now think for a moment what the benefits of an enhanced self-esteem would be to you and then list them. Be as specific as possible. If you felt great walking through the world, what kind of results would you start having in your life?

A few examples are:

I'd sleep better.

I'd have a better job.

I'd be in a better relationship.

I'd have more friends.

I'd travel more.

I'd be more comfortable in social situations.

The benefits for me of having an enhanced self-esteem are:

_____

_____

_____

_____

_____

_____

I am asked a lot about how to stay in positive thought without negative thoughts creeping back in. This can be tricky because a belief is a thought. I've been asking you to 'change your mind;' to hold more positive beliefs. The only way that I really know how to do this is through feelings. I have to get all my stories (the noise in my head that isn't true) out of the way. I don't know about you but I've been pretty attached to those stories, so that's not easy.

When you look at the last 2 lists that you have just created, what does it *feel* like? If your response is positive, you're on the right track! I believe what I feel, so to change my mind, I change my feeling and then it becomes believable... that's my evidence.

The evidence is measurable on the Vibration Meter. As you begin to feel better you will notice your vibration is higher! Give yourself a current rating:

Vibration Meter

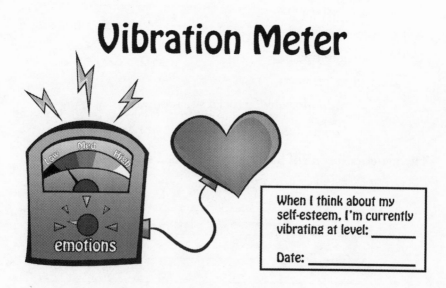

When I think about my self-esteem, I'm currently vibrating at level: _____

Date: _____

My sure fire, immediate remedy for negative thought is not earth shattering… but effective! I bring to mind all that I appreciate in my life; that I hold of value to me. My list continues to grow endlessly. It is absolutely impossible to feel bad when I am in appreciation.

If what I think about grows and becomes my reality (which is my 'truth'), then I might as well think big and set my vision high and imagine a life I can have enthusiasm about!

All feelings are fleeting; none of them last. This is both good news and bad news, depending on your perspective. Being excited can be very exhausting after a while … and what a wonderful exhaustion it is!

Thinking about that which I appreciate is easy to do anytime! Notice that when you think about these things, it is impossible to feel grumpy. When I want to change my current mood or vibration from low to higher, I simply choose to bring something to mind that I appreciate. Having a list to refer to is really helpful in particularly challenging situations.

In Section One, you started an Appreciation List and I encourage you to continue to add to it and refer to it often. It gets easier to add to all the time!

Thinking vs. Feeling

I am often asked questions like "How do I get from 'knowing' this information intellectually to really believing in myself and having positive self-esteem internally?"

This is a very great question because it means that there is an understanding of the difference between thinking "I'm great" and actually believing it. If I only think, "I'm great", without really believing in myself, I can come across as arrogant because there is a 'disconnect' from who I really am. I am only portraying an image of what I think that real self-esteem looks like, so I'm not being authentic.

It is sometimes a challenge for people who intellectualize things a lot, and the trick is to practice the art of being aware of emotions or feelings. For example, when you are proud of something you've done or accomplished, allow yourself to *FEEL* proud, not just think it.

When I feel the emotion, I know that I am in touch with my authentic self. My 'Vibration Meter' will tell me how closely I am aligned with my brilliant magnificence. In other words, having a low reading is simply good information toward choosing my direction.

On the following page there is a list of activities. Give yourself some time in between reading each one to notice how you *feel* as you imagine them. Some of these things may not feel good to you and, if that's the case, simply move on down the list.

Get comfy and, as you read each statement, allow yourself to *feel* the following 'Feel-Good Times'.

When you are through the list, you may want to add some of your own that are unique to you. Creating a great list that is personal for you will help when you are in a situation later where you want to reach for a better feeling.

Feel-Good Times

The feeling of being in love.

Laughing so hard I almost pee.

Having a hot shower.

Sharing a special glance.

Getting a personal piece of actual mail.

Taking a scenic drive on beautiful day.

Hearing a favorite song on the radio.

Lying in bed listening to the rain outside.

Being wrapped in a hot towel out of the dryer.

Having bubble bath with great music.

Giggling with my friend.

Walking bare-foot on a warm beach.

Finding a precious item I thought I'd lost.

Having a joyful water fight on a hot day.

Hearing someone tell me that I'm special.

Discovering a great connection with someone.

Holding a brand new kitten or puppy.

Having a great dream.

Having a warm drink on a winter day.

Planning a great vacation.

Accomplishing an important goal.

Special occasions spent with close friends.

Listening to a little baby giggle.

Smelling my favourite food or spice.

Offering the perfect gift to someone special.

Watching the sunset after a great day.

Feeling my favourite texture.

Listening to the crackle of a campfire.

My List of My Own Feel-Good Times

Take a moment to notice how you are feeling about yourself after doing these exercises. Give yourself another rating of your level of vibration.

Vibration Meter

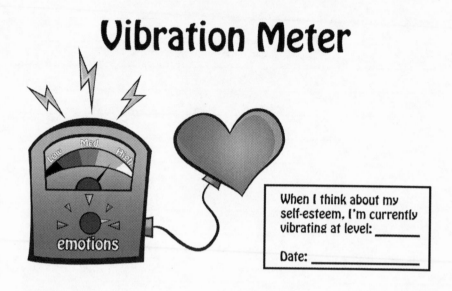

When I think about my self-esteem, I'm currently vibrating at level: _____

Date: _____

The only job you have is to feel good. The rest will handle itself. Find the value in feeling good. Figure out a way for the benefits of feeling good to out-weigh the pattern of being right about beliefs and feelings that are not effective for you.

Discover ways to continue to feel good. Find ways, especially, to feel good about YOU! Watch for and keep track of these things so that you will find evidence toward your argument for great self-esteem!

- Find a time when you did something you were proud of, or felt good about, and think about how you felt about you in that moment.
- Acknowledge yourself for all that you have done, accomplishments you have made.

- Write yourself a letter documenting the evidence that you are fabulous, even if you don't fully buy in yet.
- Start catching yourself in the act of being an amazing friend, a loving parent, offering a kindness to a stranger.

Most of us really minimize or downplay all it has taken to get to where we are in life. When I am treating people well, it's because I feel OK about me in those times. Start noticing that there is a lot of evidence to prove your own value and worth.

The more great things that I notice about my life and my experiences in it, the easier it is to notice more of them, and the more I will discover evidence of greatness!

The better I feel, the more I notice my 'good energy', and the more good energy I will attract. When I expect people to be kind, they usually are because I am putting that energy out there and noticing it.

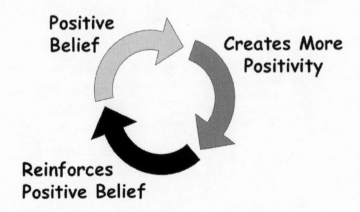

Positive Belief → Creates More Positivity → Reinforces Positive Belief

Practice 'letting it all in' and believing in your goodness.

Section 2 Assignment

The beliefs that I have about myself are formulated, often unknowingly, from cultural norms, advertisements, parents and other people of influence in our early years. With those beliefs as a framework, we treat ourselves in certain ways accordingly.

Your job now is to have a look at your current situation in life.

1. Pay attention to how you treat yourself. Do you follow through with things? Do you get good nutrition? Do you say things to others that you feel good about? Watch for more of the signs of having great self-esteem begin to show up.
2. Make sure to complete the exercises in this Section and continue to raise your awareness of your beliefs that may be getting in your way so that you can rewrite them.
3. Continue to add to your Appreciation List that you started in Section One.

When you do this, you will discover that you begin to create a new reality! The canvas is yours to paint, as you so desire!

Section 3

The Reluctant Author

Now that I am more aware of some of the stories I'm telling myself, it'll be easy to rewrite them, right? Well, that depends on how much I am really holding on to my old stories. Are you still stuck on a few of the big ones?

Most people in life (and I am certainly no exception) spend many years retelling stories about the dysfunctional aspects of their life and how they don't want it. We put a ton of effort into elaborating on brilliant, and often entertaining, versions of why I'm right where I don't want to be. Then we wonder why we continue to be dissatisfied with our results.

"But it's true," I hear people say so often. "My family was poor, my father did this, my aunt was like that, our school was too this, I didn't get to do that," and so on, and so on. "How can I not be what I am?"

I will say it again.

What I am inviting you to consider is the idea that you are, at your core (before any of your 'stories' were created) a whole, healthy, brilliant bundle of magnificent and radiant brilliance.

If this is true (and you get to decide), how can you not be what you are, regardless of any of your past? Both views are valid. One belief just doesn't work as well. You always have an option to re-evaluate what story you want to believe. I hope you choose to live the story of your magnificence.

"How do I do that? My past stories feel like they have a very strong hold on me." They absolutely can, stories are very powerful. There is, however, a difference between an experience and the interpretation you have of it.

You may have a perfectly valid reason for being right about being stuck where you are. You may even get a lot of people to validate your perspective. The problem is that, at the end of the day, it still feels miserable.

There is a way to look at your experiences in a way that serves you to move forward…

The Reframe

Without having had the negative experiences that you have had in your life, you would not have any idea what it is that you would rather have. I simply would not know concepts like 'happy' or 'fabulous' without the experience of feeling sad or horrible.

It is because I do not have money that I want it and because I do not like myself that I want to be loved. These opposing experiences are what give us the juicy preferences that we have. It would be boring if the only flavour were vanilla.

Believe It!

It is a powerful thing, to know what you want. By now you are getting clearer about what that is, and that is imperative to having it. The next step, however, is in believing that it is on its way; having faith that you will have it and begin to expect it.

I may think "I want to love myself," but if my internal response to that is a sarcastic, "Yeah, right!" then the formula isn't complete and I will not receive what I want. Our thoughts control our reality.

Given that it is difficult to control every thought that I have, an easier way to make a change is to focus on how I'm feeling, as stated earlier. The better I feel, the more believable it will be to feel good, and I will continue to expand my 'feel-good' time exponentially!

Again, practice. Say "Thank you" when someone recognizes you, not because they approve of you, but because *you* approve and you feel good about you. This isn't about depending on others to get my ego stroked - far from it. This is about relying on my own knowing about my worth; the value that has always been *me*.

It feels great to hear applause from others. If I look for validation from others to feel good, however, I also give them the power to take me down. My best and the most important validation that I receive comes from within myself; it is my own knowing that I gave something my all and that I approved!

We usually take in the criticism and the negative stuff. When I say, "Let it (compliments) in and say "Thank you," I mean remember the truth about who you are and honour yourself with that acknowledgement. My self-worth is only as great as I believe it to be. If I don't consciously believe that I have value, my unconscious mind will continue to sabotage any wishes I may have to shine or succeed. I have to believe in being the magnificent person that I am before I can become this person and show myself to the world!

Convincing myself (remembering and believing) that I am magnificent is the key to experiencing the freedom and miracle I'm looking for. Sometimes this 'convincing myself' takes practice and baby steps, and they're worth it!

Momentum to Magnificence

The 'Law of Attraction' is about building momentum. The faster a snowball rolls down a hill, the more speed and weight it gathers. Also, the better I feel about me, the better that I will feel about me.

Many people get frustrated when they are not seeing the results that they want in fairly short order. What you must realize is that you are currently manifesting results from the vibrations that you have been offering for a very long time. Even if you are feeling good more of the time, your evidence may still reflect a history of 'negative vibes'.

To stop a negative thinking pattern requires time and practice. You must slow 'your bus' down to a halt, change gears and then begin to move it in the opposite direction.

When I start heading in that good, opposite direction, I may still be tempted to think old, familiar thoughts. It's important to stay conscious of my thoughts so that I'm not detoured back down the same old road with them again. I can choose to wave, say, "Oh, hello old thought, I remember you," while continuing on my new path of alignment with my magnificence.

When it starts to feel like I'm 'in the groove,' the music is cranked up and I'm doing the 'happy dance' inside, I may notice that my bus is beginning to travel faster and faster. There are fewer and fewer detours, potholes, and distractions that will take me off my path at this rate.

Focus is fun and exhilarating… and it can be scary too. The minute I start to feel 'too good' and some fear or worry sets in (often unconsciously), is the minute when I am putting my own foot on the brake. This is the minute that I am resisting being on my path of magnificence and turning back toward struggle.

So, friends, please keep the momentum focused on your worth, on feeling good. When I do start to feel myself get worried or scared, I notice it much sooner and can adjust my course easier each time.

The more empowered I feel, the more confidence I gain, the more positive people and events I attract to me, and the better I feel!

It is one great big upward cycle of momentum!

Allow the sensation of freedom when you stay focused on feeling good. Every negative thought I may have is a diversion from my alignment with who I am and I can feel it immediately! It's not 'bad' to feel angry, frustrated, worried or any other negative emotion. Those feelings are the little warning indicator lights that come on to help me notice my momentary diversion and stay on track.

I am committed to 'checking my gauges' toward staying on my path of having the phenomenal life of abundance, health and vibrancy that I deserve!

Keep checking your meter. How's your level right now?

Vibration Meter

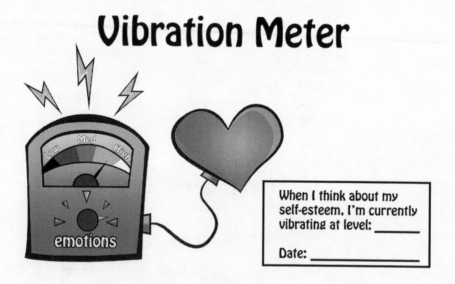

When I think about my self-esteem, I'm currently vibrating at level: _____

Date: _____

Got it! ...Oh, no, lost it again.

I've been reading and 'getting' this stuff for a long time, and it doesn't mean I've mastered it by any stretch. Just like a friend of mine says,

"Despite my belief, I seem to slip back to autopilot-thinking very easily during the course of a day, which means that often I'll catch myself having spent a good part of the time in negative/critical thinking."

"Is there a way to offset these 'accidental' negative feelings that I've put out to the universe?" "Am I now doomed to experience more tragedy?" Absolutely not! Once I 'woke up' to realize that I had 'slipped back into autopilot-thinking,' I then saw the option to simply say, "Oops, let's change that course," turn off my autopilot settings and return to thinking with conscious control.

I want to focus on what I choose, not on fixing what I don't want. The biggest irony is, if I beat myself up for being negative, I simply experience more negativity. It's just not helpful at all!

There was a time I would set a timer and give myself 5 minutes a day to give myself a lecture and get it out of my system. After that, I wasn't allowed any more. After a short time, those 5 minutes became my daily 'laugh at myself comedy routine' on how human I am.

I found a beautiful greeting card several years ago that simply reads "Be Gentle with Yourself" on the front. I took it home, framed it and hung it where I would see it each day. It is still hanging on my wall reminding me that I deserve gentleness at moments when I forget.

What If I Still Feel Frustrated Sometimes?

Now that I understand that experiencing a negative emotion is a 'good thing' because it is an indicator that I'm off track, it is helpful. There is such a thing as being 'in resistance to resistance,' however, and this can get sneaky.

I find it really helpful to name my frustration out loud (yup, I talk to myself) and say, "Wow, you really don't feel comfortable feeling good right now, do you?" When I step outside of the emotion, I have an easier time of seeing that I can change it; that I have a choice in how I feel.

There is value in feeling the shift toward positivity happen slowly over time in that it is easier to believe it or let it in. If I woke up tomorrow, after being depressed for a long time, and suddenly felt on top of the world, then I may have experienced mistrust and have the sensation that the depression will hit me again. Rebuilding my trust can take time.

I remember 'Be Gentle' and know that the results that I am currently manifesting are only a temporary sign of the path that I am on. Sometimes we can all feel like we're stuck, and movement and change are constant.

Even when I began to feel better about myself, I still got some undesirable results in my life. Please realize that the results that you are currently experiencing have manifested from an accumulation of many previous months and years of sending out the vibrational signals that you've been offering during that time.

As I began to change and send out more positive vibrations, my results also began to change. There is a 'catch up' period of time where patience and faith are necessary. My job is to continue to 'watch for the evidence' of my positive results!

'Faith' is simply another word for 'believe.' I have been inviting you to 'have faith in' or believe in your natural state of magnificence. It may not be easy to see the constant change that happens within us, yet we do grow and develop over time, whether we know it (or are aware of it) or not. Having faith or believing in my magnificence has helped to ride through that 'catch up' time, while waiting for the positive results to manifest.

As a fun exercise, imagine yourself going back to the first job that you ever had in your life. How well do you think you would fit in working there today? Notice how you have grown to be a different person than you were then.

When I am looking over my shoulder to 'what *was*,' I miss out on 'what *is*' about who I am and all that I am in this moment. If you are feeling negative emotion, then you may not be focused on the road in the direction you want to be going. Ask yourself if you are looking back over your shoulder (the past) or worrying about the road ahead (the future).

Growing Past Negativity

In the first section, you were asked to notice if you spend time complaining or retelling your old stories. Just as you remembered your first job above and saw that you don't 'fit in' at that job anymore, notice that your negative thoughts and feelings may not seem like a fit for you anymore either, although it may be a more subtle sensation.

You may notice over time that it is more and more difficult to remain negative about anything. Once I have had the realization that "I can choose to feel good" and then I began to actually believe that it's OK to feel good, then feeling bad didn't have the appeal that it used to.

Have a look at the answers that you wrote out in the last Section under "**When you imagine being completely aligned with your magnificence and you are feeling fabulous about you…**". All of those answers will be positive, affirming and will have a high-vibration feeling associated with them. The more that I imagine and feel these good sensations, the more comfortable they become and the easier they are to access. After a while, it is just plain difficult to feel lousy.

The 'Struggle Mode' Struggle

One of the main concerns I hear people report as they start to become more comfortable with feeling great is that others around them are still in 'struggle mode'. I hear things like "How on earth can I feel good when other people around me are still struggling so hard?"

It's also difficult for some to allow themselves to change their mind about 'struggle mode' being the way to get to happiness. You know, "We have to struggle and struggle or fight and fight and then, one day, we magically wake up and there will be peace, right?" As you may have figured, it doesn't work that way. The way to experience happiness is to simply stop struggling or fighting and be peaceful; be happy. That's it.

Regardless of what my own (or other people's) ideas or expectations have been about my 'feeling good state', the bottom line is that I deserve to feel good. In order to get past what others might think or feel, I am the person who must ultimately decide that there is value for me (and for every other person in my life) for me to feel good.

So, before you go any further in this book, please stop right now and look in the last section's exercise: **"When you imagine being completely aligned with your magnificence and you are feeling fabulous about you…"**

Read over the answers that you wrote down in this exercise. No, really, find it out now and flag it, **before you turn this page!**

Now that you've read over the answers that you wrote down in this exercise, think about how other people around you are being impacted in your presence when you are in this place of magnificence.

When you are radiating in the high vibration of your magnificence...

What is the general feeling that you think others might have around you?

_____
_____
_____
_____
_____
_____
_____
_____

What signs will you see that will tell you that others are drawn to you?

_____
_____
_____
_____
_____
_____
_____
_____

How do you suppose you will feel about other people, such as your family members, grocery store clerks, other drivers on the road, your co-workers?

_____

_____

_____

_____

_____

_____

_____

_____

When I feel good it's contagious. Feeling good allows others to feel OK about their own goodness. If they are not ready to choose to feel good, that's OK too.

So, how do I give permission to myself to feel good when I have thought for so long that I'm supposed to struggle? Find the value in having a positive impact! Notice how others seem to feel in your presence when you are vibrating in your magnificence. Feel the difference in your body. How can I contribute to anything but amazing results in the world when coming from my place of magnificence? Decide that it's worth it for myself AND others to be feeling amazingly great!

When I am in alignment with my magnificence, it means that I am listening to my emotions; my inner guidance system. It means that I am choosing to move toward that which feels good to me. This also means that this is true for everyone else as well. When I am feeling good, others are drawn to me and I am assisting them to move closer to their magnificence.

When I choose to feel bad and join others in their complaining or their 'struggle mode', I am reducing the odds that they will listen to their own guidance system. It's like saying, "It's OK, we can feel bad together." The message I give to others when I stay in my magnificence is, "I love you so much that I will not join you in your struggle, but call you to a better feeling place where you deserve to be."

By being happy and in alignment with my path, I attract others toward aligning with their own magnificence.

What kind of 'attraction' magnet do you want to be?

The 'Selfish' Irony

When we are taught to behave as young children, we are usually trained against listening to what naturally feels good. Children will scream in delight, want more ice cream and dance around the living room for attention, in the grocery store or when company is over.

Sometimes parents will say, "Stop being so selfish!" What they are *really* saying, ironically, is "I don't want you to do things that I am uncomfortable with." We are taught to behave 'appropriately' in all parts of society, so that other people will feel good, not so that we will. We're taught to listen to others for our guidance rather than ourselves.

Our natural guidance system of emotion is curbed and we are trained that it is 'selfish' to listen to our own cues. In fact, nothing could be so backwards. To authentically enjoy my life and have fun is the best gift I can give to others.

The next time you get the thought "How can I feel so good when others are struggling?" is the time to sit back and decide to experience joy the most! From a place of magnificence is where I see others at their best. When I see others through my lens of magnificence, they will become inspired toward their own magnificence.

Granted, joy is not always an easy choice, given that we have bonded in our struggle and often found our identity through giving up our happiness. Being joyful is a choice, nonetheless. I consider adversity or struggle to be an invitation; it's a calling to remember who I am and return to my natural best again.

Shifting the Hard Part

The trick to allowing myself to feel good is to practice feeling good. We all know how to feel good, the tough part is making it last. I hear people say that it's hard to maintain positive feelings. Here is another possible NEW reality to adopt… *feeling good is way easier than feeling lousy!*

When I'm in alignment with magnificence, it means I'm feeling energetic, light and free! Think about it. It is way easier to sing than to complain; I can feel the difference in my body. It is way easier to feel appreciation than discord. The hardest thing to experience in life is being out of alignment with my natural joy. It may simply feel more usual or habitual to be in 'struggle mode'.

All it takes to feel good, whole, free and easy is a little practice. In short order, my body said, "Wow, I remember this sensation… and I like it!" Pretty soon I was dancing around the living room with company again!

Have a blast; it's way more fun and much easier than being grumpy or worried!

Remembering

There are some strategies that I want to suggest which may help you to remember your magnificence for longer periods of time. Most folks are familiar with using affirmations. Some may say that affirmations are 'hokey,' and perhaps that's because they are missing a piece. I call affirmations '*Reminders*,' and they really work for me since I discovered the missing piece.

Repetition helps our brains to remember. When I add *feeling* to the repetitive thought, it has a significant impact on rewriting the old messages. Over time, the newer 'auto-pilot thinking' now means affirmative and magnificent thinking and I go off course only once in a while (and then for shorter and shorter periods of time).

Here are some *Reminders* on the following page that I have made up that you may find helpful. Use these, write your own, or get them from your favorite authors (Louise Hay and Marianne Williamson are great at these, to name a couple)… just find ones that you resonate with.

Choose *Reminders* that you will *FEEL* when you read them. You will know that a *Reminder* will be effective for you when you read it and you can really imagine *feeling* the experience of it in your body. Notice the statements 'amp up' in vibration as they progress down the page in the following list.

A Few Reminders:

I am in the exact place that I am meant to be in my process.

I am fully whole and complete just the way I am right now.

I fully deserve to be happy.

I am lovable and worth loving.

I am a unique and amazing person.

I have a unique light to shine on this world.

When I'm in a vibrant place, I radiate vibrancy to others and the world is brighter.

I came into this world as pure joy and when I allow my joy, I am playing my part in life's symphony.

I remember that I am a unique gift to the world; I have love to share and magic to create that only I can.

I am a whole, healthy, brilliant bundle of magnificent and radiant brilliance.

Write your own Reminders

Use the above Reminders, or find, or write your own, that you will put on your mirrors, your fridge, your screensavers, your dashboard or in your calendar. Put them anywhere where you will keep reading and feeling them. Allow them to sink in, even if you don't fully buy into them as your 'truth' yet.

_____

_____

_____

_____

_____

_____

_____

_____

_____

_____

_____

_____

Believing the bottom statement may take time. Start where it's comfortable and where you will resonate with a good feeling.

It took a lot of time to buy into the stories that you've been telling yourself since childhood, so please, cut yourself some slack! The change will come. You will begin to believe in you on a regular basis. You will feel better and it won't take forever. Start expecting this and watch for the evidence!

The Gentle Author

The story that I bought into as a child that 'I wasn't lovable' was my 'truth' for many years. My 'truth' has most definitely changed. I decided that the story was inaccurate and based on false evidence. That's right, I just decided.

It is because I learned that I could change my mind, my perceptions, my thinking (or create a new story) that I could change my reality. That is really what the Law of Attraction is: creating my own reality.

The Law of Attraction is always in effect. Whatever I give my energy (belief and focus) to, I will get more of in return. I'll get this whether it's what I may think I want, or not, *and* whether I consciously know it, or not. Since this is the case, I am now choosing to use this Law with some consciousness toward creating the positive results I really want.

Feeling bad just feels bad. Living in that place, I felt doomed and, frankly, suicidal at times. It was a place where I was in full-throttle victim thinking. To use the Law of Attraction in a conscious way toward creating a fabulous self-esteem not only feels better, I now see that I am in charge of my own life.

Today is an opportunity for you to re-author your old stories that no longer serve you or contribute to a vibrant, fabulous and magnificent life. Awareness of the old stories is helpful toward catching yourself when you are about to retell one again. This is not the time to beat yourself up, but to gently say "Oh, you sneaky story, not so fast... I'm not going to let you tell that one today!"

Get ready with your new story. Prepare yourself to present a new story of confidence to yourself. Choose to believe something different. Prepare a plan in anticipation of the old stories creeping in. Ask yourself:

"What energy do I want to vibrate out there today?"

"Will this story move me in the direction of where I want to be going?"

If it feels like work, it's not the energy to look for. Feeling good is easy and it will attract more goodness to you. We get to choose the stories we believe, what story would you rather tell yourself today?

Section 3 Assignment

1. Go through this book and complete each of the exercises.

2. Be sure to post Reminders that work for you in places where you will see them often.

3. Time yourself standing in front of a mirror for 5 full, uninterrupted minutes. Have a close look. In the first several minutes, you may notice that you will be finding all sorts of things about you that you don't like. That's fine, stay with it anyway.

   You will soon run out of those things and you will find that you will grow to be gentler with yourself. Stay there for the full time and do this exercise every day for a week. Notice that you will be looking deeper into the eyes of someone who is compassionate, caring and very worthy of your respect, love and appreciation.

   Know that you are in the presence of a magnificent friend. Expect to have this experience.

4. Write a letter of commitment to being in alignment with your magnificence. Use the attached page or choose some special writing paper of your own. This is a letter you write to yourself that you will then have at your disposal for times you may not feel so strong and confident. Be sure to point out all the advantages of alignment and remind yourself how incredible it feels.

Be sure to sign it, date it and keep it in a place where you will easily access it for later reference.

5. Notice whether you are doing all of the exercises through each Section. Are you letting time, other people or other commitments get in the way of feeling good and taking time just for you? If you are, simply notice that there may be an old belief at play that may be worth rewriting. There is nothing more important than that you feel good about you.

NOW is the time to feel Magnificent!

My Letter of Commitment to Being in Alignment with My Magnificence

_____

_____

_____

_____

_____

_____

_____

_____

_____

_____

_____

_____

_____

_____

_____

_____

_____

_____

_____

_____

_____

_____   _____

Date   Signature

Section 4

Our Ultimate Choice

Because we are made of pure and positive energy, we will return to that pure energy form when we are done here on earth (after all, energy only changes form, it doesn't end). At the end of the day, we will return to being pure energy of magnificence, no matter what. While we are here in our bodies, the choice we have on this journey is whether to feel good and enjoy ourselves along the way or whether to stay in struggle and pain.

Many of us don't always remember that we have choices in life because it can feel hard and we can feel hard done by. Think about the small feel-good moments that you've had through doing the exercises in this book. You did not have to feel good; you did because you were willing to play along. At some point, you agreed to participate in the process and, as a result, you had moments when you felt a little better.

That's what life is; moment after moment of choosing to participate in feeling good. The next time you are tempted to feel frustrated or impatient, decide how else you would rather feel and enjoy being in control of your happiness.

If you are still reading, you have made a choice to participate in feeling good. There is a part of you that knows; that really remembers and resonates with natural joy! Not everyone is willing to do this, thank you. Please continue to give the gift of this amazing choice to yourself, to me and to the rest of the world!

The Faithful Journey

The 'journey' is an interesting concept. If I am talking about a literal trip from point A to point B, it is tangible and measurable. When I know what is involved in getting to my destination, it somehow makes it easier for me to 'stay with the tour'.

This book has been about a different sort of journey. I'm suggesting that once I live in a place of feeling good about myself, I will eventually find the evidence that I am worthy of goodness; I will experience my magnificence. This process is a life journey.

If only I could know more tangibly when I am 'going to arrive' at this place of pure magnificence that I know is there for me in life, just as I know when I'm going to arrive when on a journey of a measurable distance. In the absence of this knowing, it can be easy to get impatient at times.

It would be silly to get half way home from work, come across a detour in the road, become frustrated and decide that my destination is hopeless. I would never consider turning around and going back to work (where I don't want to be) for the rest of the night. Yet, that seems to be exactly what I have done in my life at times.

The difference with the journey home from work is that I have faith that, despite the obstacles, I will arrive at my destination. This is the challenge on life's journey.

So, how long do you need to continue on the path of 'feeling good about you' before you will believe in (or have faith in) your worth and 'arrive' in your magnificence? I am suggesting that it can be just as easy to believe that you will, indeed 'arrive' here as it is to believe that you will arrive home from work the next time you take that trip.

I want to know in life, as when I'm driving from point A to B on a long trip, how long it's going to take, what it's going to cost, where I'm going to stay on the way, etc. When I don't have this information is when it seems I may lose the faith (if I had any to begin with) that I will, most certainly, arrive.

I thought, "OK, what if I just simply knew that I would arrive into my state of magnificence? What if I just believed that I would arrive there, not for moments at a time, but permanently?" Wow!

Well, it will happen, for sure, the moment that I leave my physical body and return to pure energy (because energy doesn't die), or I can choose to enjoy being in my magnificence along the journey of life today. There's no need to wait!

Since I'm here and on this journey, what's the sense in making it miserable for myself or for others? I decided that I might as well make peace with being here and use it to my advantage to have a blast!

What's the Hurry?

In our culture, I find that we do seem obsessed with 'getting there' at times. Generally speaking, we like to know things ahead of time and plan things. We like to measure outcomes and do cost/benefit analysis and research on stuff. After all, we like to prove ourselves right. Spending so much time getting it right can distract us, however, from being in 'the now.'

If I spend time in 'the now' and I love how I feel right now, does it matter how long it takes to get anywhere? Does it matter how long it takes you to get to the end of the book if you enjoy the experience of reading it?

Sometimes it can feel like the trip from A to B takes forever in a groaning, moaning kind of way. There are also times when I've travelled the same route and my experience was so stimulating and engaging that I could not believe the trip was over so fast. Since the distance was the same each time on these journeys, what explains the difference?

The only reality is the one that I create with my perception. The only difference for me on these trips is in where I choose to focus my thought and what I give my attention to.

The truth is that the journey toward my own magnificence never 'ends.' I have right now to be magnificent-feeling. How do I feel now? Then I can ask, "How do I feel now?" When I am feeling good, my 'arrival' doesn't really matter, I lose focus on worries about the future. The journey itself is the part worth savouring and enjoying along the way.

Think about the last time you wanted to rush through the most delicious meal in your life? Do you want to enjoy the lingering colours of the most glorious sunset you've ever seen, or do you want the sun to just hurry up and disappear? When you are in the middle of the sweetest kiss with your lover, do you think to yourself "Oh, hurry up!"? It is the moment itself that is sweet; it is not about 'getting somewhere.'

Savour the knowledge that you know how to feel good and your results will be there. Recognize the evidence of feeling good right now… and right now, and now.

Some people spend so much time and energy wanting to feel worthy and never get there because they are focused on why they are not worthy. We can stay focused on justifying and arguing all the reasons why we either cannot feel good, why we don't or on why we won't. If you believe these conditions are so, then they shall be so. It is as true as the old saying, "Whether you think you can or you think you can't, you're right". And, you do get to choose what to be right about.

Resisting Resistance

It is difficult to allow yourself to be happy and feel good when you are feeling bad. Worse than that, however, is being upset at yourself for feeling bad when you think you should know better. Goodness knows I've been in this vicious cycle!

When you have mastered the art of 'allowing' your magnificence and feeling good now, you are not resisting anything. If you look at something that you don't like and you resist it (meaning, give energy to it or focus on it), you are denying yourself your moment of joyous magnificence.

This doesn't mean there are no unpleasant things in the world, it means that to focus on them will attract more of them in the future and take you away from the moment that you deserve now.

If you resist the idea of poverty, issues of politics, religion, or personal opinions that you don't like in others, then you are going to discover more of those negative feelings about those issues. You are not vibrating good, high energy in those moments and that vibration will perpetuate your negative vibration, amplifying your discomfort with the issue.

The trick is to be in harmony; aligned with your positive vibration of magnificence regardless of what you hear or see around you. Whether you are in the middle of an argument that others may be having or seeing a homeless person on the street, whatever the situation is, if you are feeling good about who you are and are focused on that, you will eventually discover that you are in unpleasant situations far less frequently. You have mastered the art of allowing your magnificence and the world will respond to your vibrational state.

When others are in discomfort, it does not mean you need to be. You can be more supportive, helpful and influential in improving their vibrational state by remaining in your own high vibration. This takes practice. This takes faith. You will find the evidence that this is so the longer you sustain your high vibrational state.

Remember to Appreciate the Contrast

One of the ways that you can stay in a positive vibration while others are not is to appreciate the experience of the contrast between your vibrations. When you hear or see something you don't want, it helps you to identify what you do want. Look at that which is unappealing and smile in appreciation of it for helping you to identify what is pleasing to you.

Enjoy the contrasting experience because it is the gift that tells the universe what it is you want. You would not have gotten to the place of feeling good without the contrasting feeling that you experienced before.

Re-Authoring Beliefs About Support

One thing that appears to be difficult for most people to do is ask for help. Somewhere along the line, we created beliefs like, "I have to do everything on my own", or "It's a sign of weakness to ask for help," and so on. If these beliefs sound familiar to you, you may want to do some re-authoring here.

Bring to mind the people that you have had the most respect and admiration for throughout your life. Who are your mentors? They may be historic figures, social activists, super-heroes, politicians, or perhaps your friends, family members, or old teachers and coaches that you've had.

What kind of qualities do they have that you admire in them? Are these people who you would imagine to have a good self-esteem? Would you describe them as confident? Do you see them as a leader?

Any good leader is a person who knows how to ask for help. (I don't know of a great leader who got to be in their position all on their own.) Anyone who wants to have a positive impact on the world knows how to utilize support from others.

To be willing to ask for support requires some degree of good self-esteem. I must feel worthy of receiving the gift of other people's time and resources as well as having a willingness to accept their gifts because I deserve it.

The key to this is that it really isn't all about you. What I mean is that people usually really want to help and like to be asked to give it. You could be missing an opportunity to help someone feel valued and appreciated. It's fabulous that while you are accepting help and support from people, you are helping them to increase their self-esteem at the same time!

If I approached you and said to you, "I'm working on a project and I was thinking about you and your incredible ability to *(fill in the blank)*, and I'm wondering if you would be willing to offer me some support with your skills?," how do you think you would feel?

Feels rather nice, doesn't it?

An important part of asking for help is being willing to hear 'no' for an answer. People don't even need to give me a reason why they say no. This does not mean that I get to have an excuse to feel bad about anything. It means I have great people in my life who know their limits. Cool!

Having the courage to ask people for their help and support does several magical things:

- I am contributing to someone else feeling good about their value.
- It says to them, "I see you" and they feel recognized.
- It says to them, "It's OK for you to ask for help from me too."
- It gives me an opportunity to hear "Wow, I'd be happy to be associated with you," which is very affirming.

o   I get better results when utilizing others' skills and resources.

o   I feel a sense of connection rather than isolation.

o   I am not stagnating; I am willing to take risks to get what I want in life.

o   I get to build more and more confidence.

o   I create stronger friendships and connections.

o   I will help others practice boundary setting by letting them know that 'no' is a perfectly acceptable answer.

Now, here's an opportunity for you to think about how you can increase these benefits in your life. Give some careful consideration to the exercise on the following page.

My Support People

Make a list of the people currently in your life who are truly supportive of you being in alignment with your magnificence:

_____

_____

_____

_____

_____

_____

Make a list of people you know who you think could be on the above list, if you asked them for support:

_____

_____

_____

_____

_____

_____

Decide whose self-esteem you would like to positively impact. Consider adding their names to the second list. When you feel really good about you, does it make it easier to ask for help? You certainly deserve all the help you can get, in all areas in your life. If that sounds foreign to you, here is another reminder (affirmation) to consider:

For those who are in your life who are not supportive, don't focus on them. Don't let these people become a reason to stop your momentum. Focus on those who do support you and support these people, as you want to be supported yourself.

On the following page there is a 'Support Plan' included to get you started on consciously creating a magnificent support team in your life.

My Magnificent Support Plan

The person that I am willing to share what I have learned (in this book) with is:

_____

Their Name

I will contact this person to schedule a time to meet with them by: *(within the next 3 days is preferable)*

_____

Date and Time

What I'd like them to know about me (as a result of me reading this book) is:

_____

_____

_____

_____

_____

_____

The kind of support that I will ask this person for from now on is:

(For example, would you like regular phone calls or email 'check-ins'? How often? Be really specific.)

_____

_____

_____

_____

_____

_____

_____

In Review

After working through this book, these are some of the beliefs that you may now hold about what you have accomplished:

- I am now consciously using the principles of the Law of Attraction to create and experience greatly enhanced self-esteem.
- I have identified and changed some old beliefs and I have written (and will continue to write) new ones that serve me far better.
- I understand that my feelings have a vibrational energy, which creates my results, and I have tools that will always help me to get in a higher vibration.
- I have gotten more clearly in touch with who I am in my magnificence and have experienced what it feels like being there.
- I have begun an 'Affirmation List', which I can add to, begin or end my day with or refer to when I would like a boost.
- I have created *'Reminders'* (affirmations) that resonate with me, *feeeel* good, and work for me.
- I live more consciously in the present moment than I have before; I understand it's a practice.
- I have hard evidence of my true magnificence.
- I know that I am having an amazingly positive impact on the world and those around me.
- I have created a plan to experience great support on my magnificent journey.
- I experience life with a new sense of excitement and passion in my magnificence.

The longer I stay on this magnificent path, the more and more evidence I will find that I am living a new and improved life. I will continue to notice that:

- I count on myself as a 'friend.'
- I have improved relationships at home, at work... and everywhere.
- I feel more attractive and attract more positive people to me.
- I have more energy, enthusiasm and zest for life.
- Others treat me better and I treat myself better.
- Life feels easier; I sleep better and have more fun.
- I am a more effective problem solver and I manage stress easier.
- The profoundly positive impact that I have on the world reaches further than I had ever imagined.
- I feel deserving of love, joy and laughter and experience more of these each day.
- The 'goose-bump' experience becomes a regular part of life; it is becoming my dominant vibration.

Give yourself a huge pat on the back! Relax in the knowing that you 'have arrived' and that this moment is the most important moment there will ever be. Like me, your great self-esteem will be more solidly present and accessible to you through the ups and downs of life than you once believed possible.

I know that I am brilliant energy regardless of what others think or say! Anything that I hear to the contrary simply means that others are not in alignment with their own magnificence. I never have to wait for 'one day' or for someone else to be different in my life to be happy. I can always choose to be happy now!

In Summary

I am, at my core, a whole, healthy, brilliant bundle of magnificent and radiant brilliance. I know this and know how to access it and feel it. Any negative emotion that I feel is there only because I am in resistance to being in touch with (or in alignment with) my magnificence. No exceptions.

When I experience something that is unwanted, I can automatically put into motion that which I do want by vibrating an energy, which the universe will then respond to.

The circle is complete.

One of my greatest challenges is to stop being so adamantly right about why I am not where I want to be. When doing so, I rip myself off from allowing in all the joy that is waiting for me. I don't feel the joy because I am too busy telling stories about why I can't get there or why I can't have it.

Any moment that I am looking at the past or worrying about the future is a moment that I am not allowing myself to feel good now. When I practice feeling good now, I continue to feel better and better all the time. I see incredible evidence of my results!

When I feel great about me and am in alignment with my magnificence, I love what I do, generate fabulous abundance, have amazing friends, experience joy and passion in all I do and have a relaxed approach to all of life's challenges. I am set for life!

Whatever I want is here for me to receive. When I feel good about me and I am in alignment with my magnificence; the world is my oyster!

Section 4 Assignment

1. Complete all of the exercises that you may not have completed in the book to date.

2. Complete the '**Next Steps**' sheet, included on the following page.

3. Remember to keep checking your Vibration Meter. How's your level right now?

Vibration Meter

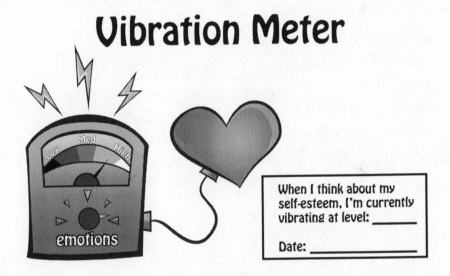

When I think about my self-esteem, I'm currently vibrating at level: _____

Date: _____

No matter where you are, remember that you can always reach for a better feeling thought!

My Next Steps

You now have a full book of material to refer to during times when you feel stuck. Remember it and keep it handy. Go over it again and again to remind yourself how to realign with your magnificence.

Consider developing and committing to a magnificent routine, which will incorporate some of the tools covered here. For example:

Activity	Time of Day	Completed
Review My Appreciation List	_____	☑
Read & *Feeel* a 'Reminder' (an appreciation) or 2	_____	☐
Check My Vibration Meter	_____	☐
Find evidence of at least 1 "Sign of Positive Self-Esteem"	_____	☐
Read My Commitment Letter	_____	☐

Also, choose an 'old belief' that may still be getting in your way (i.e. a belief about relationships, money, etc.). Write a 'New' belief that serves you better and commit to finding evidence of it this week.

My 'old' belief is:

_____

_____

My 'New' belief is:

_____

_____

_____

Your Signature

Sandy's Favorite Authors, Suggested Readings & Greatest Influences

Jerry & Esther Hicks – The Teachings of Abraham.
They have many books, DVD's, YouTube videos, recordings of their
conferences and more. They are the driving influence behind
the words in this book.

Randy & Judy Revell – founders of Context Associated
The Excellence Series courses, which changed my life.

Eckhart Tolle – Author and Spiritual teacher
'The Power of Now', 'A New Earth' & 'Stillness Speaks', and his work
with Oprah in their webcast course 'A New Earth'

Lynn Grabhorn – Author
'Excuse Me, Your Life Is Waiting – The Astonishing Power of Feelings'

Byron Katie – Author and Creator of 'The Work'
The most effective strategy to 'Loving What Is' imaginable!

Michael Losier – Author, Facilitator & Coach
'The Law of Attraction – The Science of Attracting More of What You
Want and Less of What You Don't'

Janet & Chris Attwood – Authors & founders of 'The Passion Test'

Sonja Johnson – Feminist Activist and Author
'Going Further Out of Our Minds' speech in the early 80's

There are simply too many more to mention…

NAMASTE

Sandy Slovack, MA, is a Registered Clinical Counsellor, Inspirational Speaker, and Workshop Facilitator who lives in Courtenay, B.C., Canada.

To join Sandy's mailing list and see further resources, visit:

http://www.SelfEsteemSolutions.com

To contact Sandy, email:

Sandy@SelfEsteemSolutions.com

Printed in the United States
By Bookmasters